The *Easy* Baseball Book

by JONAH KALB
The *Easy* Baseball Book

illustrated by SANDY KOSSIN

Houghton Mifflin Company Boston

Also by JONAH KALB

The Kids' Candidate
How to Play Baseball Better
Than You Did Last Season

Library of Congress Cataloging in Publication Data

Kalb, Jonah.
    The easy baseball book.

    SUMMARY: Discusses ways of improving baseball
techniques, how and where to practice, how to choose
equipment, and how to make simple equipment to
improve skills.
    1. Baseball — Juvenile literature. [1. Baseball]
I. Kossin, Sandy. II. Title.
GV867.5.K33 796.357'2 75-44085
ISBN 0-395-24385-8

Text copyright © 1976 by Jonah Kalb
Illustrations copyright © 1976 by Sanford Kossin

BP 10 9

To all the kids, and former kids,
who find, in baseball,
the anchor of their early years.

Introduction

This book doesn't tell you
how to play baseball. After all,
you already know how to play baseball.

This book just tells you
some of the little things
that even very good players
sometimes forget.

Also, even very good players sometimes
get into slumps.
They can't seem to hit the ball,
or they start missing easy catches.

It happens to major league players,
so it probably happens now and then
to you, too.

Knowing the little things can
help you get back to
your real ability.

So this is a book
of the little things:
how to hit;
how to field;
how to throw;
how to practice;
how to check yourself.

HITTING

Equipment

You already have some equipment.
You probably have a ball and a bat.

Be sure to get a batting helmet.
A helmet protects your head.
Get one with ear flaps
to protect the sides of your head.

The next time you buy a bat,
be sure to get one light enough
to swing quickly.

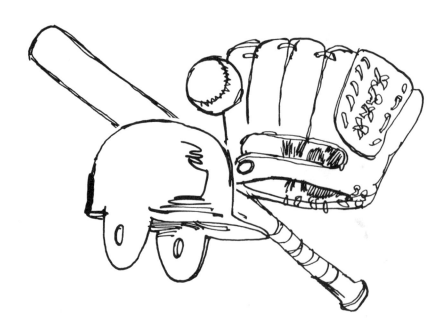

Look on the knob of the bat.
A number 7 means that the bat is
27 inches long; a number 8, that it is
28 inches long.
One of these should be about right.

Longer bats weigh more
and are hard to swing quickly.

Buy a wooden bat.
Aluminum bats cost a lot
and you will be changing bats
as you get bigger.

Never try to bat without your helmet.
And never try to swing a bat
that is too heavy for you.

Getting Ready to Hit

You already know how to get
ready to hit. This is just a check
list in case you forget something.

If you are right-handed,
grip the bat with your right hand
over your left hand, about one inch
above the knob. Like this:
Hold the bat over your right shoulder.

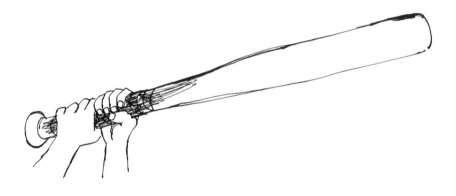

If you are left-handed,
grip the bat with your left hand
over your right hand.
Hold the bat over your left shoulder.

Face the side of the plate.
Place your feet about one foot apart.
Bend your knees.
Point your front shoulder at the pitcher.
Shift most of your weight
to your back foot.

Keep your elbows away from your body.
Keep the bat off your shoulder.
Turn your face to the pitcher
so that you can watch him
with both eyes.

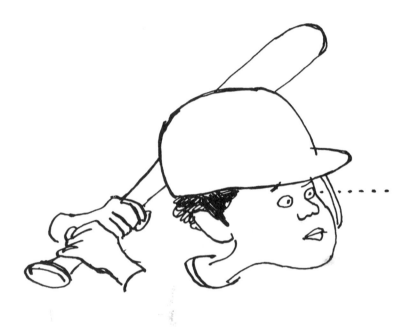

Watch the pitcher. Watch the pitcher.
Watch the pitcher.

You are now ready to hit.

How to Hit

You already know how to hit.
But you may miss more than you'd like.
Here is what to keep in mind.

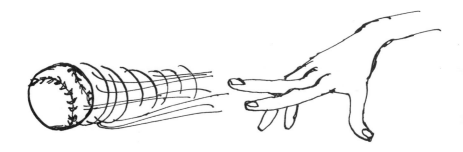

Watch the pitcher. When the pitcher
throws the ball, watch the ball.
See if you can watch the ball
all the way to the bat.
Keep your eyes open,
even if you are scared.

When you swing, keep your back foot
in place. Step with your front foot
right at the pitcher. Turn your hips
toward the pitcher as you swing.

Swing the bat as if you are
throwing the fat part of the bat
right at the pitcher's chest.
(But don't let go.)
That will keep your swing level.

Swing all the way around,
even if you miss the ball.
This is called "follow-through."
You get power and distance
from follow-through.

Common Mistakes and How to Fix Them

Here are some mistakes many kids make.

They swing too slowly. They swing
after the ball has already passed them.
They should choke up on the bat.
That means, move their hands
four or five inches above the knob.

If they are still swinging too late,
they should get ready
by pointing the bat right at the catcher.
This will shorten the swing.

If they are swinging too high, they
should try to swing lower next time.

If they are swinging high one time,
and low the next time,
and just missing all the time,
they are probably closing their eyes.

It is okay to be afraid.
Even major league players are afraid
of getting hit by the pitch.

But closing their eyes won't help.
If they get hit by the ball
it will still hurt (a little).
But they have to watch the ball.

The "Dos" and "Don'ts" of Hitting

Do get ready before you swing.
That means, get your hands right,
your feet right, your body right,
and watch the pitcher.

Do get the bat on the ball.
Nothing else really matters.

Do step and swing with one motion.
With a lot of practice,
you will find that this motion
of your whole body together
is easy and natural.

Do swing level.
Do follow through.

Don't swing too hard.
Don't close your eyes.
Don't step "in the bucket."
Step right toward the pitcher.

Don't swing at bad pitches.
Nobody hits bad pitches very well.
A good pitch is one that is
over the plate, between your arm pits
and your knees.

Don't swing your head when you
swing the bat. Keep watching the ball.

Don't get down on yourself.
Hitting well is very hard.
It takes a lot of practice.

How to Practice Hitting

Everybody needs to practice.
Even good hitters need to practice.

Have a pitcher throw to you.
Mom, dad, sister, brother, or
a friend would be just fine.
Wear your batting helmet.
Have them pitch easy at first.

To practice by yourself,
get a plastic ball with holes.
Throw the ball up and hit it.
The ball won't go very far
because of the holes,
so you won't have far to chase it.

Build a few batting tees
at different heights. A batting tee
is a piece of broomstick
stuck in the ground, with six inches
of rubber hose on top.
You put a baseball on the top
of the rubber hose, and swing.

In the winter, you can
hang a ball of yarn from a pipe
in your basement. Be sure
you have lots of room to swing.
Change the height of the ball
now and then. Practice. Swing.

FIELDING

Equipment

You probably already have
a baseball cap with a peak.
The peak keeps the sun
out of your eyes, and makes you
feel like a baseball player.

You probably also have a glove.
The best glove to have now is
a fielder's glove — with five fingers.
You can play more positions with
a fielder's glove than with a catcher's
mitt or a first baseman's mitt.

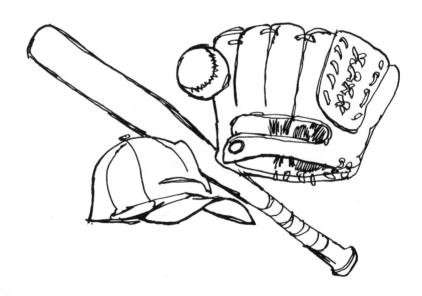

A right-handed player gets a glove
for his left hand.
A left-handed player gets a glove
for his right hand.

When you are buying a glove,
put your hand into the glove
so that you can still see
all of your wrist sticking out.
Then open and close your hand.

A good glove should close fairly
easily when you close your hand,
and should open by itself when
you relax your hand.

Getting Ready to Field

You already know how to catch.
You already know, therefore,
that it is important to be ready.

Baseballs are almost never hit
right at the fielder.
The fielder almost always has to
move in or out, left or right.

As you know, the best way
to be ready is to face
the batter. Stand with your feet
apart, as far apart as the width
of your shoulders. Bend your knees.
Lean forward a bit.

If you are playing infield,
hold your hands loosely
in front of you, near the ground.
Keep your glove open, facing the batter.

If you are playing outfield,
rest your hands loosely
on your knees.

Be alert. Watch the hitter.
Watch the ball.

How to Field
Ground Balls

Of course you already know that
when fielding a ground ball
you run to get your body
directly behind the ball.
You do not field a ground ball
to the side unless you have to.

Keep your glove open, facing the ball,
and low. Keep your head down.
Use both hands. Watch the ball
all the way into your glove.

If you have time, move in
on the ground ball. Don't wait
for the ball to reach you.
Move in and meet it.

This is called "charging the ball."
Infielders always charge when they can.

Expect bad bounces. Be ready for them.
You will probably never play
on a field that isn't filled with
stones and holes.

How to Field
Fly Balls

Sure you already know
how to field fly balls.
But here are some reminders.

Run as fast as you can
to where you think the ball
will land. Then wait for it.

If you have to, you can then
move in a little, or over a little.

Get behind the ball if you can.
It is easier to move in
than move out.

Line the ball up on your nose.
Catch it in front of your face.
Use two hands.

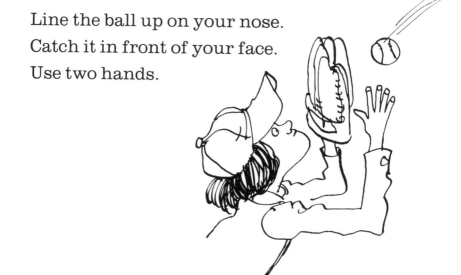

If the ball is hit behind you,
turn around, run back,
turn around again,
and catch it in front of you.

Don't pedal backwards.
Nobody can run fast that way.

Watch the ball all the time
it is in the air.
Even when you turn around to run,
watch the ball over your shoulder.

Common Mistakes and How to Fix Them

Here are a few common mistakes
some players make.
If ground balls are getting through, they
are probably bouncing under the glove.

The players are probably lifting their
heads before they have the ball, too.

They should keep their gloves low,
even on the ground sometimes.
They must watch the ball
all the way into the glove.

Like hitting, it's okay to be afraid,
but a player has to keep
his eyes open and his glove low.

On fly balls, if players run
to the right place, but still
miss the ball, they are probably
taking their eyes off the ball
in that last second.

If players don't know where
the ball is coming down, they
just need more practice.
Judging fly balls is very hard.

The "Dos" and "Don'ts" of Fielding

You already know all this but
do get ready before every play.
Do bend your knees. Keep your
glove open, hands low.

Do watch the ball.
Do run fast and wait, instead of
running slowly and just meeting
the ball. Charge ground balls.

Do catch with both hands.
Do get your body behind the ball.
Do keep your glove low. Low.

Don't lift your head until you
have the ball in your glove.

Don't take your eyes off the ball.
Don't catch to the side.
Don't pedal backwards. Turn around,
run, then turn around again.

Don't worry about being afraid.
You can be a good player anyway.

How to Practice Fielding

Even good players
have to practice fielding.
The best practice is to get somebody
to hit baseballs to you.
Get your partner to hit easy ground
balls first, then harder and
harder ones. Get him to hit to your
right and to your left.

If you can practice on pavement
(a parking lot on a Sunday
is a good place), use a tennis ball.
Your partner can hit with
a tennis racket.

By yourself, throw a tennis ball
against your garage door or a wall.
Catch it. When this becomes too easy,
throw harder, or stand closer, or both.

Get someone to hit fly balls
with a tennis ball and tennis racket.
They are easy to hit that way.

Throw a ball up by yourself,
circle under it, and catch it.

Play catch with anyone who will
play with you. A friend who is
also practicing is perfect.

THROWING

Equipment

You already have a baseball.
Sooner or later, you will lose it
and you will buy another one.
This is what you should know
about baseballs.

The best "hitting" baseballs are covered
with leather. They are best for games.
Leather baseballs, however, scuff easily,
just like your leather shoes.
They become dirty, and after a while
they are hard to see
against a background of trees.
If they get wet, they get heavy.

Vinyl-covered baseballs look and feel
like leather baseballs, but they can
be washed. They stay white longer, and
they don't soak up water.

Rubber-covered baseballs can be
washed and don't soak up water either.
They are also very sturdy.

The best practice baseballs,
therefore, are either rubber- or
vinyl-covered baseballs stamped
"Official Little League."

Getting Ready to Throw

You already know how to throw.
If you learn how to throw well,
and if you have a strong arm,
you probably can become a pitcher.
That's a lot of fun.

Grip the ball correctly.
Put your thumb under the ball,
and your first two fingers
on top of the ball.
Hold the ball with those fingers only.
Your last two fingers just rest.

Grip the ball firmly, but do not
squeeze it. Put your first two
fingers on the seams of the ball.

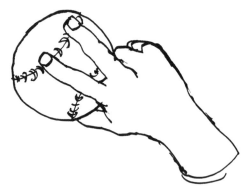

You must get your whole body
ready before you throw.

If you are right-handed, stand sideways
with your left foot in front of your
right foot. Point your left shoulder
in the direction of your throw.

Raise your right hand, holding the ball
behind your right ear. Cock your wrist.
Look at your target.

Now you are set.

Left-handed players do the same thing
with the opposite shoulder, hands, and feet.

How to Throw

Put your weight on
your back foot.
If you are right-handed,
point your left toe straight
at your target and step with
your left foot.

At the same time, move your
throwing hand quickly forward,
and pull your left hand back.
Pretend you are "giving the ball"
to your catcher.

When your throwing hand is stretched
in front of you, flip your hand down.
Let the ball slide off your fingers.

After the ball is thrown,
don't stop your natural movement.
Keep moving your whole body.
Bend your back. Raise your back foot.
Keep watching your target.
Like swinging around when you hit,
this is called "follow-through."

All this action should be done
as smoothly as possible.
It is really all one motion,
as you know.

Left-handed throwers do the same thing
except the hands and feet are opposite.

Common
Mistakes
and How to
Fix Them

Some players who don't throw so well
"push the ball" from near their chins.
They should throw from behind the ear.

If the throws are always too low,
they are probably stepping out
too far with their front foot.
They should take a shorter stride.

If the throws are always too high,
they are not stepping out far enough.
They should take a longer stride.

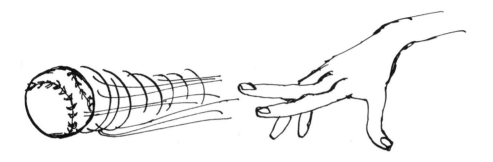

If they are always missing the target
on the right, or on the left,
they are probably not pointing the
shoulder and the toe directly at
the target.

If they are always throwing wild,
they may be gripping the ball
the wrong way, or throwing when they
are not really ready. They should
go through all the steps
of getting ready.

The "Dos" and "Don'ts" of Throwing

You know all this,
but it's good to check yourself.

Do throw "overhand," from
behind your ear. "Sidearm"
throws are usually wild.

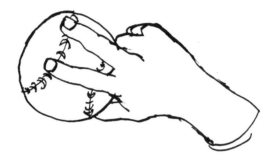

Do grip the ball correctly.
Always get set before you throw.

If you pick up a ground ball
and are off balance, stand up,
get set, then throw.

Don't throw without getting ready.

Don't throw for too long
at one time. Throwing too much
will give you a sore arm,
a sore shoulder, and a sore elbow.

Most important,
never throw at all if there is
soreness in the arm, shoulder, or elbow.

Never twist your wrist when throwing
to try to get a curve ball.
Twisting the wrist can hurt your arm
and that's not the way to throw
a curve ball anyway.

Throwing well takes a lot of practice.

How to Practice Throwing

Playing catch with someone else
is good throwing practice,
and good catching practice, too.
After a while, back up to about
90 feet. That's as long a throw as
you will have to make until you are
about thirteen years old.

Get your partner to roll some
ground balls to you. Pick them
up and see how quickly you can
throw hard and straight.

Throwing a tennis ball against a garage
door or a wall is also good practice.
Mark a 2-foot-by-2-foot square
on the door or wall with masking tape.
Use a clean tennis ball.
Try to throw the ball into the square.

If you can get it in the square
every time, stand farther back,
or make the square smaller.

You might want to cover the square
with wrapping paper.
That way, you will hear it
every time you hit the square.

Practice, practice, practice.

Dreaming

This book doesn't tell you
how to dream.
You have to figure that out
for yourself.

But dreaming about baseball —
daydreaming and night dreaming —
is one of the best parts
of the game.

In our dreams, each of us
can make the impossible catch;
each of us can throw
the perfect pitch;
each of us can slide home in the
last inning with the run
that wins the game
and wins the pennant.

Each of us can be a hero,
at least to ourself, even if
it is only in the secret places
of our mind.

Each of us can hear
the roar of the crowd.

Baseball is that kind of game.
You can dream about it.
And the dreams can make you happy.

Baseball is a game you can love.